KIDS ON EARTH

Wildlife Adventures – Explore The World
Arctic Fox - Iceland

Sensei Paul David

COPYRIGHT PAGE

Kids On Earth: Wildlife Adventures - Explore The World

Arctic Fox - Iceland

by Sensei Paul David,

Copyright © 2023.

All rights reserved.

978-1-77848-169-7 KoE_WildLife_Amazon_PaperbackBook_Iceland_arcticfox

978-1-77848-168-0 KoE_WildLife_Amazon_eBook_Iceland_arcticfox

978-1-77848-374-5 KoE_Wildlife_Ingram_PaperbackBook_ArcticFox

This book is not authorized for free distribution copying.

www.senseipublishing.com

@senseipublishing
#senseipublishing

Synopsis

This book is a collection of 30 unique and fun facts about the Arctic Fox in Iceland. From their diet and behavior to their habitat and more, the book provides an insight into the lives of these incredible creatures. It covers topics such as their fur color, diet, habitat, and more, and provides interesting facts about the Arctic Fox and its importance in the Icelandic culture. Whether you are 6 or 12 years old, this book is the perfect way to learn more about the Arctic Fox. So, let's dive in and explore these fascinating animals!

Get Our FREE Books Now!

kidsonearth.life

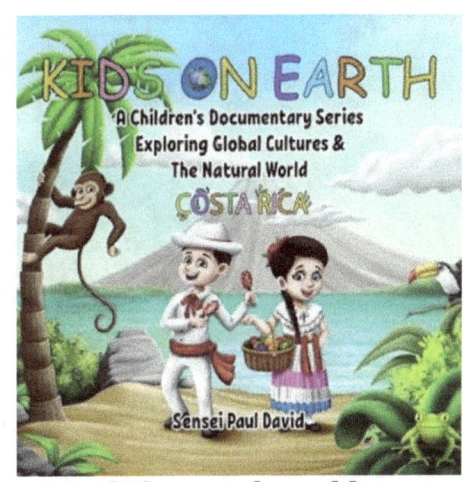

kidsonearth.world

Click Below for Another Book In Each Series

senseipublishing.com/KoE_SERIES

senseipublishing.com/KoE_Wildlife_SERIES

KoE En Español

senseipublishing.com/KoE_SERIES_SPANISH

www.senseipublishing.com

Join Our Publishing Journey!

If you would like to receive FUTURE FREE BOOKS and get to know us better, please click www.senseipublishing.com and join our newsletter by entering your email address in the pop-up box.

Follow Our Blog: senseipauldavid.ca

Follow/Like/Subscribe: Facebook, Instagram, YouTube: @senseipublishing

Scan the QR Code with your phone or tablet to follow us on social media:

Like / Subscribe / Follow

Introduction

Welcome to the world of the Arctic Fox! This book is a collection of 30 unique and fun facts about the Arctic Fox in Iceland. From their diet and behavior to their habitat and more, this book is sure to teach you something new about these incredible creatures. Whether you are 6 or 12 years old, this book is the perfect way to learn more about the Arctic Fox. So, let's dive in and explore these fascinating animals!

The Arctic Fox is a small white fox native to the Arctic regions of the Northern Hemisphere, including Iceland.

The Arctic Fox mainly feeds on lemmings, voles, birds, eggs, fish, and insects.

The Arctic Fox has thick fur to help keep it warm in its cold environment.

The Arctic Fox has a thick tail which helps it balance when walking on snow and ice.

The Arctic Fox has an amazing ability to hear and locate prey up to 1km away.

The Arctic Fox has a unique adaptation of changing its fur color to white in the winter and brown in the summer to better blend in with its environment.

The Arctic Fox is an excellent hunter and is able to capture prey even under thick snow.

The Arctic Fox is a solitary animal and mostly lives alone.

Arctic Foxes have small ears that help minimize heat loss.

The Arctic Fox has a high reproductive rate and can have up to 10-12 pups in a litter.

They are solitary hunters and do not rely on pack tactics to catch prey.

The Arctic Fox is a very adaptable animal and can survive even in areas with very little food.

The Arctic Fox is an important part of the Icelandic culture and has been featured in many traditional stories and folklore.

The Arctic Fox is an important predator in its environment and helps to keep the populations of other animals in balance.

The Arctic Fox has been known to travel up to 30km in a single day in search of food.

The Arctic Fox is a very curious animal and will often investigate anything new in its environment.

The Arctic Fox has a thick fur coat and is able to withstand temperatures as low as -58 degrees Fahrenheit!

The Arctic Fox has an excellent sense of smell and can detect food up to 1 mile away.

The Arctic Fox is an intelligent animal and has been known to use tools to find food.

The Arctic Fox is a nomadic animal and will travel great distances in search of food.

The Arctic Fox is an incredibly agile animal and is able to jump up to six feet in the air.

The Arctic Fox is a popular subject for wildlife photographers, who often go to great lengths to get the perfect shot.

The Arctic Fox is a protected species in Iceland and is strictly monitored by the authorities.

The Arctic Fox is a symbol of resilience, being able to survive in one of the harshest environments on Earth.

The Arctic Fox plays an important role in the local ecology and helps to maintain the balance of the food chain.

The Arctic Fox is an important part of the Icelandic economy and is hunted for its fur.

The Arctic Fox has a unique ability to store fat in its tail which helps it survive long periods without food.

The Arctic Fox is a loyal animal and there have been reports of foxes staying with their owners for many years.

The Arctic Fox is a friendly animal and has been known to be very curious and approach humans.

The Arctic Fox is a mesmerizing animal and watching its movements in the snow is an unforgettable experience.

Conclusion

The Arctic Fox is a fascinating creature that is full of surprises. From its diet and behavior to its habitat and more, this book has taught you 30 unique and fun facts about the Arctic Fox in Iceland. We hope you have enjoyed learning more about these incredible animals and that you are inspired to learn even more.

Thank you for reading this book!

If you found this book helpful, I would be grateful if you would **post an honest review on Amazon** so this book can reach other supportive readers like you!

All you need to do is digitally flip to the back and leave your review. Or visit <u>amazon.com/author/senseipauldavid</u> click the correct book cover and click on the blue link next to the yellow stars that say, "customer reviews."

As always...

It's a great day to be alive!

Share Our FREE eBooks Now!

kidsonearth.life

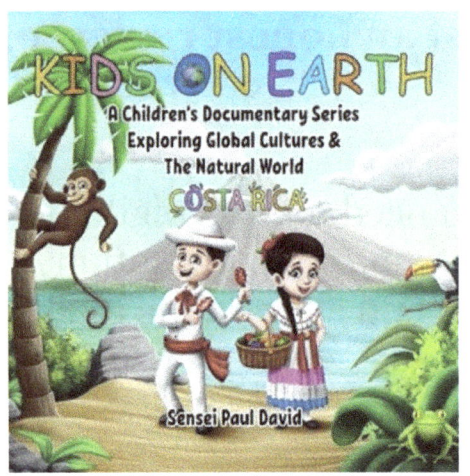

kidsonearth.world

Click Below for Another Book In Each Series

senseipublishing.com/KoE_SERIES

senseipublishing.com/KoE_Wildlife_SERIES

KoE En Español

senseipublishing.com/KoE_SERIES_SPANISH

www.senseipublishing.com

www.senseipublishing.com

@senseipublishing
#senseipublishing

Check out our **recommendations** for other books for adults & kids plus other great resources by visiting
www.senseipublishing.com/resources/

Join Our Publishing Journey!

If you would like to receive FREE BOOKS and special offers, please visit www.senseipublishing.com and join our newsletter by entering your email address in the pop-up box

Follow Our Engaging Blog NOW!
senseipauldavid.ca

Get Our FREE Books Today!

Click & Share the Links Below

FREE Kids Books
lifeofbailey.senseipublishing.com
kidsonearth.senseipublishing.com

FREE Self-Development Book

senseiselfdevelopment.senseipublishing.com

FREE BONUS!!!
Experience Over 25 FREE Engaging Guided Meditations!

Prized Skills & Practices for Adults & Kids. Help Restore Deep Sleep, Lower Stress, Improve Posture, Navigate Uncertainty & More.

Download the Free Insight Timer App and click the link below:
http://insig.ht/sensei_paul

About Sensei Publishing

Sensei Publishing commits itself to help people of all ages transform into better versions of themselves by providing high-quality and research-based self-development books with an emphasis on mental health and guided meditations. Sensei Publishing offers well-written e-books, audiobooks, paperbacks, and online courses that simplify complicated but practical topics in line with its mission to inspire people toward positive transformation.

It's a great day to be alive!

About the Author

I create simple & transformative eBooks & Guided Meditations for Adults & Children proven to help navigate uncertainty, solve niche problems & bring families closer together.

I'm a former finance project manager, private pilot, jiu-jitsu instructor, musician & former University of Toronto Fitness Trainer. I prefer a science-based approach to focus on these & other areas in my life to stay humble & hungry to evolve. I hope you enjoy my work and I'd love to hear your feedback.

- It's a great day to be alive!
Sensei Paul David

Scan & Follow/Like/Subscribe: Facebook, Instagram, YouTube: @senseipublishing

Scan using your phone/iPad camera for Social Media
Visit us at www.senseipublishing.com and sign up for our newsletter to learn more about our exciting books and to experience our FREE Guided Meditations for Kids & Adults.

www.ingramcontent.com/pod-product-compliance
Lightning Source LLC
Chambersburg PA
CBHW080617110526
44587CB00040BB/3733